Public Procurement. EU Court rulings 2023

Robert Myhre

Robert Myhre

PUBLIC PROCUREMENT

EU COURT RULINGS 2023

#

Publisher: BoD · Books on Demand, Postboks 354 Sentrum, 0101 Oslo, bod@bod.no
Print: Libri Plureos GmbH, Friedensallee 273, 22763 Hamburg, Tyskland

ISBN: 978-82-845-1227-3

Introduction

This book compiles nine of the most interesting and significant rulings
from the Court of Justice of the European Union (CJEU) in 2023
concerning public procurement.

The purpose of the book is to provide a practical and accessible
review of these decisions, focusing on how they impact the practices
of public contracting authorities, suppliers, and other stakeholders
operating within the framework of EU law.

I hope this book will serve as a valuable resource for anyone seeking
to understand how the CJEU enforces the fundamental principles of
transparency, equal treatment, and proportionality, and how these
principles are translated into concrete solutions in practice.

Oslo, January 2025

Robert Myhre

Innholdsfortegnelse

1. C-403/21, Judgment of 26 January 2023

- - Interpretation of special legal requirements into the tender documents
- - Rejecting a bidder for failing to disclose subcontractors in advance

I. THE ESSENCE OF THE CASE

The case concerns whether a contracting authority can require suppliers to meet obligations derived from special legislation, even when these obligations are not explicitly stated in the tender documents. Furthermore, it examines whether a bidder can rely on the capacity of another entity without formalizing this through a subcontracting agreement.

II. FACTS OF THE CASE

The case pertains to an open tender in Romania for technical services related to road construction, announced by the Timiş County Council. The contract value exceeded the thresholds set out in Directive 2014/24/EU. NV Construct, which placed fourth in the competition, challenged the compliance of the top three bidders, arguing they failed to meet requirements not specified in the tender documents but mandated by special Romanian legislation.

Tender Requirements:

The tender documents outlined technical and legal requirements for suppliers but did not include specific approval requirements from

national authorities, such as the Romanian Railway Authority
(Autoritatea Feroviară Română).

Claimant's Allegations:

NV Construct alleged that the top three bidders lacked the necessary
approvals from national authorities as required under Romanian
special legislation. They also argued that the selected bidder, which
relied on the capacity of other entities, should have formalized this
cooperation as a subcontracting agreement under Romanian law.

Contracting Authority's Defense:

The contracting authority claimed it was impossible to know at the
submission stage whether specific activities, such as preparing
expropriation documentation, would be necessary. They argued that
such requirements could be fulfilled during the implementation phase
and that there was no need for subcontracting agreements or specific
approvals at the submission stage.

Selected Bidder:

The selected bidder indicated that they, or others as needed, would
obtain the required approvals after contract award.

Core Conflict:

The issue was whether the contracting authority could impose specific
requirements from special legislation that were not explicitly
mentioned in the tender documents. Additionally, it addressed
whether a bidder could rely on another entity's capacity without
formalizing the relationship as subcontracting.

The ruling thus examined the balance between the need for clarity in tender documents and the flexibility afforded to suppliers in meeting requirements during contract execution.

III. THE COURT'S ASSESSMENT

The CJEU assessed the case under Directive 2014/24/EU, focusing on Article 58 (qualification criteria), Article 63 (use of others' capacity), and the fundamental principles of equal treatment, transparency, and proportionality.

1. Interpretation of Qualification Criteria (Article 58)

Requirements Must Be Included in the Tender Documents:

- The Court held that contracting authorities have flexibility in defining qualification criteria, but these must be proportionate, adapted to the nature of the contract, and clearly stated in the tender documents.
- Implicit requirements based on national legislation cannot be enforced unless explicitly outlined in the tender documents. Suppliers must have the opportunity to know and prepare for all applicable requirements to ensure equal treatment.

2. Interpretation of Using Others' Capacity (Article 63)

Formalizing Cooperation:

- The Court ruled that Article 63 does not mandate that bidders must use subcontractors when relying on another entity's capacity. Bidders have the flexibility to choose how to meet the requirements, whether through collaboration, subcontracting, or other legal arrangements.
- It was unnecessary for the selected bidder to name subcontractors for tasks that might not even be performed.

3. Principle of Transparency

Clarity in Tender Documents:

- The Court emphasized that tender documents must be clear and predictable to ensure transparency and fair competition. If special requirements from national legislation are not specified in the tender documents, they cannot later be used to exclude suppliers.

4. Principle of Proportionality

Assessment of Special Requirements:

- The Court stated that special requirements from national legislation, such as specific approvals, may be included in tender documents as qualification criteria or contract performance conditions. Such requirements must be necessary and reasonably related to the contract's objectives.

5. Timing of Fulfilling Requirements

- The Court accepted the contracting authority's argument that certain requirements, such as specific approvals, could be fulfilled during the implementation phase of the contract, making it unnecessary to require them at the submission stage.

III. PRACTICAL IMPLICATIONS FOR PROCUREMENT OFFICIALS

Clear and Precise Tender Documents

Formulation of Requirements:

- Tender documents must specify all requirements for suppliers, including any special requirements derived from national legislation.
- Failure to mention such requirements in the tender documents may prevent the contracting authority from excluding suppliers who do not meet them.

Recommendation:

- Conduct a legal review of tender documents to ensure all relevant requirements are included, either as qualification criteria or performance conditions.

Timing of Requirement Fulfillment

Flexibility in Fulfillment:

- Requirements that only become relevant during the contract's implementation phase do not need to be qualification criteria at the submission stage.
- This allows suppliers to obtain necessary approvals or certifications later in the process.

Recommendation:

- Assess whether requirements for approvals and certifications can be fulfilled in later phases, especially if they are not critical for bid evaluation.

Use of Others' Capacity

No Obligation for Subcontracting:

- Suppliers can rely on another entity's capacity without formalizing the relationship as subcontracting.

- Contracting authorities must accept alternative forms of cooperation, such as agreements or other legal arrangements, instead of mandating specific subcontracting agreements.

Recommendation:

- Ensure tender documents allow flexibility in how suppliers meet requirements, without limiting it to a single form of cooperation.

Reduced Risk of Complaints

Avoid Surprising Requirements:

- Contracting authorities must avoid excluding or disqualifying suppliers based on requirements not clearly stated in the tender documents.
- This reduces the risk of complaints and legal disputes from suppliers.

Recommendation:

- Communicate requirements and evaluation criteria clearly to ensure all suppliers understand what is expected and how bids will be evaluated.

Proportionality and Transparency

Adaptation of Requirements:

- Qualification criteria must be proportional to the contract's objectives and necessary to ensure fair competition.

Recommendation:

- Evaluate each requirement to ensure it is relevant, reasonable, and suited to the nature of the contract.

Handling National Special Legislation

Collaboration with Authorities:

- If national legislation imposes specific requirements affecting the tender documents, contracting authorities should collaborate with relevant authorities to ensure proper integration of these requirements.

Recommendation:

- Include national special requirements as clear qualification criteria or performance conditions in the tender documents.

VI. ANALYSIS

Can special national legislation not explicitly mentioned in the tender documents ever justify excluding suppliers if it was not communicated during the tender phase?

- According to the CJEU's findings in this and similar cases, the general answer is no. The principles of transparency, equal treatment, and predictability require that all requirements suppliers must meet be clearly specified in the tender documents.
- If special legislation pertains to fundamental public interests, such as national security or public health, the contracting authority may argue that suppliers must still meet these requirements. However, this must be assessed on a case-by-case basis, and the requirements must be evidently necessary to lawfully execute the contract.

How can suppliers be provided with clear guidance on meeting requirements not explicitly mentioned in the tender documents?

- Contracting authorities should include in the tender documents details on how suppliers can ask questions and where answers will be published.
- They may attach documents or guidelines outlining how suppliers should address special legislation or requirements that may become relevant during contract execution.
- Contracting authorities can specify that certain requirements only apply during the implementation phase of the contract and not as qualification criteria. This must be communicated clearly to ensure suppliers understand what is required and when.

2. C-682/21, Judgment of 26 January 2023

- Rejection of a supplier – Requirement for individual assessment
- Contradiction in being placed on a "blacklist"

I. THE ESSENCE OF THE CASE

The case addresses whether Member States can implement rules that automatically place members of an economic consortium on a list of unreliable suppliers following the breach of a public contract.

II. FACTS OF THE CASE

An economic consortium of companies was awarded a contract for constructing a healthcare building in Vilnius, Lithuania. The contract was later terminated due to substantial deficiencies, including delays, lack of on-site supervision, and failure to provide insurance.

As a result, all members of the consortium were automatically added to a list of unreliable suppliers, barring them from participating in future public tenders for three years. The members argued that their individual liability was not sufficiently assessed and that automatic listing was disproportionate.

The practice in Vilnius was challenged on the grounds that it failed to provide suppliers with an opportunity to defend themselves before the decision and contravened the principles of proportionality and individual assessment outlined in EU Directive 2014/24. Lithuania's Supreme Court referred questions to the CJEU for clarification on interpreting the directive in this context.

III. THE COURT'S LEGAL ASSESSMENT

1. Individual Assessment

The CJEU ruled that Member States cannot implement practices where all members of a consortium are automatically deemed unreliable after a contract breach.

- Requirement: Each assessment must be concrete and individualized.
- Implication: Only those members directly linked to the breach or who failed to take necessary corrective measures can be excluded.

2. Principle of Proportionality

The grounds for exclusion must align with the principle of proportionality.

- There must be a reasonable relationship between the behavior of the economic operator and the consequences for that operator.

3. Right to Challenge

The Court emphasized that Member States must ensure effective remedies.

- Each member of a consortium has the right to contest the decision to list them as unreliable suppliers.

4. Self-Cleaning Measures

Economic operators must be given the opportunity to demonstrate corrective actions taken to address previous failures and restore their reliability.

Consequences

A practice that automatically excludes all members of a consortium without individual assessment is incompatible with the EU directive.

This ruling reinforces the requirement for individualization and proportionality in evaluating unreliable suppliers and affirms suppliers' rights to fair treatment and effective remedies.

IV. IMPLICATIONS FOR PROCUREMENT OFFICIALS

1. Individual Assessment of Suppliers

- Procurement officials must evaluate each supplier or participant in a consortium separately when assessing reliability.
- Automatic exclusion of all consortium members based on collective responsibility is not permitted.

2. Evidence and Documentation

- Procurement officials must have robust systems to document which actions are attributable to specific members of a consortium.
- This includes gathering evidence to substantiate decisions to exclude one or more actors.

3. Facilitation of Self-Cleaning

- Procurement officials must provide suppliers linked to breaches an opportunity to explain themselves and present measures they have implemented to correct previous errors.
- A transparent process for evaluating self-cleaning measures can reduce the risk of complaints and legal challenges.

4. Increased Administrative Burden

- The requirement for individualized assessments and the right to challenge decisions will require more time and resources to ensure thorough and well-documented evaluations.

5. Right to Effective Remedies

- Procurement officials must prepare for suppliers to challenge decisions they perceive as unfair.
- This may require establishing systems to ensure decisions are reviewable and justifiable.

Summary

This judgment imposes stricter requirements on procurement officials to ensure fair treatment of suppliers by mandating individualized assessments and transparency. Although it increases the administrative burden, it also strengthens trust in the procurement process and reduces the risk of legal conflicts. It encourages better supplier quality by rewarding actors who take responsibility for past errors and improve their reliability.

V. FURTHER QUESTIONS

Threshold for Exclusion of Individual Consortium Members

To exclude an individual member of a consortium, their actions must:

- Have a direct and significant impact on the breach.
- Display intent or gross negligence.
- Not be corrected through sufficient self-cleaning measures.
- Be deemed severe in relation to the nature, scope, and purpose of the contract, justified in accordance with the principle of proportionality.

How Can Procurement Officials Evaluate the Effectiveness of Self-Cleaning?

Documentation Requirements:

- Obtain detailed evidence from suppliers about corrective actions implemented, such as:
    - Internal audit reports.
    - Confirmation from independent oversight bodies.
    - Copies of new internal policies or guidelines.
    - Evidence of staff training or certification.
    - Information on organizational changes, such as replacing management or key personnel.
- Require a detailed explanation of how the measures will prevent future errors or breaches.

Independent Verification:

- Engage third-party auditors or experts to verify the measures implemented by the supplier, ensuring objectivity.
- Contact previous contracting authorities who have worked with the supplier post-implementation of self-cleaning measures to assess improvements.

Follow-Up:

- Require regular reporting from suppliers on the status of their corrective actions, especially in high-risk sectors.
- Conduct periodic inspections or audits to ensure adherence to self-cleaning measures.

Analysis of Recurrence:

- Monitor for signs of repeated issues, such as unethical behavior or contract breaches.

Proportional and Context-Specific Evaluation

- Assess whether the implemented measures are relevant and proportional to the supplier's previous errors.
- Evaluate whether the measures are fully implemented or still in the planning stage.

Embed Control Mechanisms in Contract Terms

- Include audit clauses in contracts to allow for inspections and reviews of compliance with self-cleaning measures.
- Define consequences for non-compliance, including the potential for future exclusion.

By incorporating these measures, procurement officials can ensure robust evaluations and maintain the integrity of the procurement process.

3. C-53/22, Judgment of 9 February 2023

I. THE ESSENCE OF THE CASE

This case examines whether a supplier who has been excluded from a public procurement procedure can retain a legal interest in challenging the award decision based on competition law principles, even after their exclusion has been finalized by a court ruling.

II. FACTS OF THE CASE

Background

The regions of Lombardy and Liguria initiated a public tender for the provision of helicopter rescue services, with an estimated value exceeding €200 million. The tender required suppliers to hold a specific certification as a minimum eligibility criterion.

Parties Involved

- VZ: A supplier excluded for failing to meet the minimum certification requirement.
- RT and BO: The winning suppliers, later accused by VZ of participating in an anti-competitive cartel.

VZ's Exclusion

VZ contested the certification requirement but lost in Italian courts. The exclusion of VZ became final, disqualifying it from further participation in the procurement procedure.

Challenge to the Award Decision

After its exclusion, VZ alleged that the remaining bidders (RT and BO) had engaged in a cartel agreement, warranting annulment of the award decision and a new tender process in which VZ could potentially participate.

Key Question

The central issue was whether VZ, despite its finalized exclusion, could still have a legal interest in challenging the award decision based on alleged anti-competitive behavior by the other bidders.

III. THE COURT'S LEGAL ASSESSMENT

1. Right to Challenge (Article 1(3) of Directive 89/665/EEC)

- The Court emphasized that the right to challenge award decisions is limited to parties with a genuine interest in securing the contract.
- Once a supplier's exclusion is finalized, they no longer qualify as an "interested party" and lose the right to challenge the award decision.

2. Status of Excluded Suppliers

- A supplier that is temporarily excluded and actively contesting its exclusion may retain the right to challenge the award decision.
- However, in cases where the exclusion is finalized, as with VZ, the supplier is no longer part of the competitive process and cannot reopen its legal interest based on claims of anti-competitive behavior by others.

3. Allegations of Anti-Competitive Behavior

- VZ argued that the cartel agreement between the remaining bidders undermined the competition and invalidated the award decision.
- The Court dismissed this claim, holding that a finalized exclusion prevents the supplier from using allegations of anti-competitive behavior to regain standing in the procurement process.

4. Competition Law Precedents

- While anti-competitive behavior is a serious concern, such matters should be addressed by other participants or relevant competition authorities.
- Excluded suppliers cannot circumvent their exclusion by raising competition law issues post-exclusion.

5. Principle of Legal Interest

- The Court reaffirmed that the complaints system is intended to resolve genuine disputes concerning rights and interests in the procurement process.
- If a supplier has no possibility of winning the contract, there is no legal interest to justify their complaint.

Conclusion

The CJEU ruled that VZ, whose exclusion had been finalized, no longer had a legal interest in challenging the award decision, even on the grounds of alleged anti-competitive behavior by other bidders. The right to challenge is reserved for parties with a realistic chance of securing the contract.

This decision aligns with the principle of efficiency in complaint systems, ensuring that such procedures are not used to advance hypothetical or speculative claims from parties no longer part of the competition.

IV. IMPLICATIONS FOR PROCUREMENT OFFICIALS

This decision clarifies important principles regarding legal interest in public procurement. The Court emphasized the need for efficiency and predictability in procurement processes, which means that entities that have been definitively excluded cannot re-enter the competition with new arguments. At the same time, the decision may be perceived as strict for entities uncovering illegalities after their exclusion.

Consequences for practice:

1. Clear Boundaries for Excluded Suppliers

- Procurement officials can rely on the principle that excluded suppliers cannot re-enter the competition after a finalized exclusion to challenge award decisions.

2. Importance of Timely Arguments

- Suppliers must present all relevant arguments before their exclusion becomes final.

3. Limitation of Risks

- The principle of finality reduces the risk of unnecessary delays in procurement procedures caused by speculative claims from excluded suppliers.

V. FURTHER QUESTIONS

Would the Outcome Be Different if the Exclusion Were Not Finalized or Still Under Appeal?

Yes, the outcome could differ if the exclusion were not finalized or under active appeal. The CJEU has previously recognized that temporarily excluded suppliers may retain the right to challenge award decisions if their appeal could potentially reinstate them into the competition.

This is based on the following principles:

Temporary Exclusion

If the exclusion is not legally binding, the entity may still have a real opportunity to be reinstated in the competition if their appeal is successful. In such cases, the entity remains "affected" by the award decision and thus retains the right to challenge it.

Right to Legal Review

Article 1(3) of Directive 89/665/EEC on review procedures grants entities the right to effective legal remedies against decisions affecting their interests. A provisional exclusion later found to be unjustified could have allowed the entity to win the contract, and therefore, they should be able to challenge the award decision.

Principle of Legal Certainty

The principle of legal certainty implies that an entity should have the opportunity to challenge decisions that may have affected their ability to participate in the competition. This includes both the exclusion decision and any errors in the award decision.

Practical Implications

If an entity has a pending appeal against exclusion, contracting authorities may need to consider this appeal before finalizing the contract award. In such cases, the contracting authority must balance the need for efficiency in the process with ensuring that all entities are treated fairly.

<u>Summary:</u>

If the exclusion was not legally binding or the entity had a pending appeal, they could have a legitimate legal interest in challenging the award decision. This is because the outcome of the appeal against exclusion could potentially have allowed them to continue in the competition. This underscores the importance of fair and transparent processes in public procurement.

How can contracting authorities handle allegations of competition violations from excluded entities, especially when such allegations may affect the legitimacy of the competition?

When excluded entities make allegations of competition violations, contracting authorities face the challenge of balancing the legitimacy of the competition with the efficient execution of the process. Here are some approaches contracting authorities can use:

<u>Clear Delineation of Excluded Entities' Rights</u>

- Confirm the Exclusion's Legal Validity: Contracting authorities should first ensure that the exclusion is legally valid, and that the excluded entity therefore has no right to challenge the award. This reduces the risk of delays in the process.
- Separate Assessment of Competition Violations: Even if an excluded entity cannot directly challenge the award decision, their allegations of competition violations can be reviewed separately to ensure the process's legitimacy.

  o

Involvement of Relevant Authorities

-   Reporting to Competition Authorities: If plausible allegations of collusion exist, contracting authorities should inform relevant regulatory bodies with the expertise and mandate to address such issues.
-   Coordination with Regulatory Authorities: Contracting authorities should cooperate with competition authorities to ensure that allegations are handled promptly and effectively, without unnecessarily delaying the procurement process.

Documentation of Assessments

-   All assessments should be thoroughly documented to ensure transparency and enable subsequent review.

Proportional Measures

-   Interim Measures: If the allegations seem serious, contracting authorities may consider temporary measures, such as delaying the contract award until a preliminary review is conducted.
-   Proceeding with Reservations: If the allegations do not immediately appear well-founded, contracting authorities may choose to continue the process, with the caveat that competition authorities could later alter the outcome.

Does the contracting authority have the right to process a complaint, even if the complainant lacks legal standing?

Contracting authorities may choose to process a complaint even if the complainant formally lacks legal standing, but this depends on the national rules and principles governing complaint handling in the relevant   country.

However, certain considerations and principles can guide contracting authorities in such situations:

- A complaint without legal standing should typically be dismissed to maintain efficiency and avoid delays. This is especially important in public procurement, where swift and definitive decisions are necessary to maintain process continuity.
- If the complaint contains serious allegations, such as corruption, competition violations, or breaches of fundamental principles, it may be appropriate to process the complaint to ensure the process's legitimacy.
- If the complaint reveals potential errors that could harm the process's integrity, the contracting authority can use the complaint as the basis for an internal assessment without necessarily providing formal processing.

-   Justification for why a tender is not abnormally low

I. THE ESSENCE OF THE CASE

This case examines the extent of the contracting authority's duty to provide a justification when allegations of abnormally low bids are raised and the level of transparency required in sharing the evaluation with bidders.

II. FACTS OF THE CASE

<u>Background</u>

The European Commission issued a framework agreement for IT services for the Directorate-General for Taxation and Customs Union (TAXUD). The tender was divided into two lots and evaluated based on the best price-quality ratio, requiring both quality and economic sustainability.

For Lot A, the Commission received two bids:

1. A joint bid from ARHS–IBM, which was ultimately awarded the contract.
2. A bid from the S2U companies (Sopra Steria Benelux and Unisys Belgium), which was not selected.

<u>Award Decision</u>

ARHS–IBM achieved the highest overall score, driven by its lower price, resulting in a favorable price-to-quality ratio. The S2U companies challenged this decision, arguing that ARHS–IBM's bid was suspiciously low and should be investigated as potentially abnormally low.

The S2U companies requested the Commission to justify why ARHS–IBM's bid was not considered abnormally low. They contended that the offered price was unreasonably low given the project's complexity and risks, highlighting concerns about "social dumping," where labor and wage conditions might not comply with legal standards.

Commission's Response

The Commission rejected the claim, providing a brief explanation. It stated that a financial analysis confirmed the bid aligned with market conditions in the relevant countries. However, the Commission did not provide details of the analysis or the specific elements reviewed.

III. THE COURT'S ASSESSMENT

Legal Framework

Under Article 170(3) of the Financial Regulation and Point 23 of Annex I, contracting authorities must, upon request, inform a bidder in writing about:

- The "qualities and relative advantages" of the winning bid.
- The reasons why the winning bid was not considered abnormally low, if explicitly asked.

Key Findings

Obligation to Provide Detailed Justification

The Court emphasized that the contracting authority cannot rely on vague assurances, such as stating the bid "meets market conditions." When a rejected bidder raises concrete concerns about an abnormally low price, the authority must provide a detailed explanation of why the bid was deemed sustainable.

Outcome

The Court upheld the principles applied by the General Court, concluding that the Commission's brief explanation was insufficient. The appeal by the Commission was dismissed, reinforcing the obligation to provide a thorough and transparent justification when allegations of abnormally low bids arise.

IV. ANALYSIS

Strengths of the Judgment

- Clarity on Obligations: The decision clarifies that contracting authorities must offer substantive explanations when bidders raise specific concerns about abnormally low bids.
- Enhanced Legal Protections: This strengthens the rights of rejected bidders and ensures accountability in procurement decisions.

Weaknesses of the Judgment

- Increased Administrative Burden: Authorities must now invest more time and resources in analyzing and documenting pricing evaluations when challenged.

Practical Implications

For Contracting Authorities:

- Be prepared to provide detailed justifications for why a bid is not considered abnormally low, especially if explicitly requested by a bidder.
- Ensure that pricing evaluations include documentation of compliance with labor and wage laws, tax regulations, and market conditions.

For Rejected Bidders:

- Clearly and specifically raise concerns about abnormally low pricing to trigger a more detailed response.
- Use the information provided to assess whether the winning bid was lawful and prepare for potential appeals.

Relevance to National Procurement Practices

<u>Based on the Procurement Directives:</u> The EU's Financial Regulation (2018/1046) primarily applies to the EU institutions' own procurements but is largely based on the same principles as the procurement directives (2014/23/EU, 2014/24/EU, 2014/25/EU). The purpose is to ensure that the EU institutions' own tenders adhere to standards similar to those imposed on Member States.

<u>Not identical wording, but the same principles:</u> The text of the Financial Regulation is not a verbatim copy of the directives, but Article 161 makes it clear that any updates should be harmonized with changes to the directives. The key competition and transparency requirements – and the definition of abnormally low bids – are practically very similar.

<u>Interpretation influences national practice:</u> Rulings on the Financial Regulation provide guidelines on how EU public procurement law is interpreted. Although they formally apply only to the EU institutions,

they often "mirror" the logic of the directives. National contracting authorities, which implement similar (or the same) rules, therefore cannot disregard these principles.

<u>Abnormally low bids as a good example:</u> Both the Financial Regulation and the directives refer to "abnormally low" as a potential reason to reject a bid. The core concepts are the same: the risk of social dumping or underpricing, and the inability to execute the contract under the stated conditions. The Court's reasoning on the type of justification and documentation required is thus equally relevant for national authorities.

Consequences for Future Tenders

Improved Documentation:

Contracting authorities must improve the documentation of their evaluation processes to demonstrate the sustainability of low bids.

Enhanced Rights for Bidders:

Rejected bidders are entitled to meaningful explanations to evaluate the legality of award decisions.

V. CONCLUDING COMMENTS

The judgment clarifies that a contracting authority cannot merely refer to an "immediate" assessment that the bid is not abnormally low but must provide a genuine justification if the supplier explicitly requests it.

Although the regulation applies directly to EU institutions, the judgment highlights principles that national contracting authorities must also consider – because the rules in the directives and the Financial

Regulation mirror each other. Consequently, the risk of having an award decision invalidated is greater if a sufficient explanation is not provided to demonstrate that a low bid is indeed feasible under the applicable requirements.

5. T-376/21, Judgment of 14 June 2023

I. THE ESSENCE OF THE CASE

The dispute revolved around two primary issues:

- Whether the European Commission fulfilled its duty to provide adequate reasoning for its evaluation of the bids.
- Whether the rejection of documentation provided via hyperlinks was justified, particularly when such information could have influenced the quality assessment of Instituto Cervantes' bid.

II. FACTS OF THE CASE

Background

The European Commission launched a tender for framework agreements on language training services for EU institutions. The tender aimed to establish parallel framework agreements, ranking the two best bids as primary and secondary contractors.

Award Criteria

The tender documents specified that bids would be evaluated based on the most economically advantageous offer, with the following weighting:

- Price (30%)
- Quality (70%), assessed based on subcriteria including teaching methods, instructors' qualifications, online resources, and organizational solutions.

Evaluation Results

1. CLL Consortium: Ranked first, scoring higher than Instituto Cervantes on both quality and price.
2. Instituto Cervantes: Ranked second, with lower scores due to specific deficiencies, including reliance on hyperlinks for some documentation.

Use of Hyperlinks

Instituto Cervantes did not upload all required documentation directly through the eSubmission platform, as specified in the tender documents. Instead, they included hyperlinks to external websites containing information relevant to the quality criteria (e.g., teaching methods and resources).

The Commission rejected the hyperlinks, citing the requirement that all documentation be uploaded directly to ensure immutability and equal treatment of bidders.

Commission's Justification for the Award Decision

- The CLL Consortium scored higher overall, with better performance on the pedagogical, organizational, and resource-related subcriteria.
- Instituto Cervantes received lower scores due to the rejection of hyperlink-based documentation and the assessment that ist solutions were less effective than those of the CLL Consortium.

The justification provided included the point distribution between the bidders, which reflected the assessed differences in quality and price. The Commission considered the justification sufficient to meet the transparency requirements.

III. THE COURT'S ASSESSMENT

The justification provided included the point distribution between the bidders, which reflected the assessed differences in quality and price. The Commission considered the justification sufficient to meet the transparency requirements.

1. Rejection of Hyperlinks in the Bid

The Court upheld the Commission's decision to reject hyperlink-based documentation, reasoning:

- Tender Requirements: The tender documents explicitly required all documentation to be uploaded through the eSubmission platform. This ensured that submitted materials were immutable and accessible at the time of submission.
- Equal Treatment of Bidders: Hyperlinks introduce the possibility of post-submission alterations, undermining the principle of equal treatment.
- Proportionality: The rejection of hyperlinks was proportionate, as bidders were clearly instructed to upload all documentation directly.

2. Duty to Provide Reasoning

The Court assessed whether the Commission's justification for the award decision met transparency requirements:

- Reasoning Requirements under EU Law: Contracting authorities must provide reasoning detailed enough to enable bidders to understand why their offer was not selected and to assess whether to challenge the decision.

- Use of Point Scores: The Court found that the provision of point scores, reflecting differences in quality and price, sufficiently explained the evaluation outcome.
- No Obligation for Detailed Subcriteria Explanation: The Court clarified that authorities are not required to provide a detailed breakdown of each subcriterion, provided the overall explanation, including scores and general observations, is adequate.

3. Proportionality Principle

The Court also reviewed whether the rejection of hyperlinks and the corresponding downgrading of Instituto Cervantes' bid adhered to the principle of proportionality:

- Strict Application of Formal Requirements: The Court emphasized that contracting authorities have discretion to enforce formal requirements to ensure fairness in the procurement process.
- No Disproportionate Impact: The rejection of hyperlinks was deemed a necessary and legitimate measure to ensure compliance with the tender requirements and equal treatment.

IV. ANALYSIS

Strengths of the Judgment

- Clarity on Formal Requirements: Confirms that contracting authorities can require all materials to be submitted directly and reject hyperlinks to safeguard evaluation integrity.
- Enhanced Transparency: Ensures that bidders receive sufficient reasoning to understand the evaluation process and outcome.

Weaknesses of the Judgment

- Rigidity in Documentation Submission: May limit bidders' ability to present innovative or supplementary resources hosted externally.

Practical Implications

1. For Contracting Authorities:
   - Clearly state in tender documents that all materials must be submitted directly, specifying that hyperlinks may not be considered valid.
   - Ensure transparency in evaluation by providing point scores and a general explanation of differences between bids.

2. For Bidders:
   - Avoid relying on hyperlinks for critical documentation unless explicitly permitted.
   - Ensure all necessary information is uploaded directly to the submission platform to comply with formal requirements.

Relevance for National Procurement Practices

1. General Principles Apply:
   - Although this case concerns EU institutions, its principles reflect general procurement rules under EU directives and national laws, such as equal treatment, transparency, and compliance with formal requirements.
2. Discretion to Define Formalities:
   - The ruling reinforces the broad discretion of contracting authorities to establish and enforce submission requirements.

Is it sufficient to provide only scores in the justification?

- It is not correct to say that the court has ruled it is always sufficient to provide only scores as a justification for an award decision.
- The court clarifies that scores alone can be sufficient, provided they offer enough information to understand the evaluation decision and allow tenderers to assess the basis for a potential complaint.

<u>Scores can fulfill the duty of justification if:</u>

- The award criteria and scoring clearly illustrate the differences between the offers.
- The evaluation does not raise issues requiring further explanations (e.g., specific weaknesses in an offer).

<u>The court found that in this case, it was sufficient to refer to:</u>

- The scoring distribution
- The explanation regarding hyperlinks
- The superior fulfillment of requirements related to pedagogical methods and organization by the winning tenderer

Is it always prohibited to accept bids with hyperlinks?

The court's assessment indicates that it is safest to avoid the use of hyperlinks for documentation critical to the evaluation, unless:

- The tender documentation specifies strict rules for the use of hyperlinks.
- Technical mechanisms are in place to ensure the hyperlinks cannot be altered.

When can hyperlinks be accepted?

- When the content cannot be altered: If it can be documented that the hyperlinks point to static files that cannot be modified after submission, this may be a safer alternative.
- When the links are secondary: Hyperlinks can be used as supplementary to the required documentation, but not as the primary source of critical information that is directly evaluated.

What should be included in the tender documentation?

- Clear regulation of hyperlinks: The tender documentation must specify that hyperlinks are only accepted if they meet specific technical requirements, such as immutability or access verification.
- Alternative requirements: Procurers should allow tenderers to upload the necessary documents directly onto the platform as a standard and avoid reliance on external links.

6. C-601/21, Judgment of 7 September 2023

I. ESSENCE OF THE CASE

This case addresses whether Poland's national legislation, which allows direct awards of contracts for the production of sensitive documents (e.g., ID cards, passports, and ballots) to a state-owned company without open competition, is compatible with EU procurement rules. The key question is how the principles of competition and equal treatment should be balanced against Member States' rights to protect their essential security interests.

II. FACTS OF THE CASE

Background

Poland introduced a law permitting the direct award of contracts for the production of sensitive documents to its state-owned enterprise, Polska Wytwórnia Papierów Wartościowych S.A. (PWPW). The justification was that these documents are critical to national security.

The European Commission's Claim

The Commission alleged that Poland violated its obligations under Directive 2014/24/EU by bypassing open procurement procedures. The Commission argued that Poland could protect national security through less restrictive measures within the directive's framework.

Poland's Defense

- Security Measures: Poland argued that producing sensitive documents requires specific security measures that cannot be ensured through regular tendering procedures.
- Risk of Leakage and Insolvency: Poland claimed that private suppliers could expose the country to risks such as forgery, data leaks, and the insolvency of contractors.

The Commission's Counterarguments

- Alternative Measures: The Commission argued that risks could be mitigated by setting strict security requirements in the tender process, including standards for confidentiality, technical capacity, and financial stability.
- Proportionality: The Commission contended that Poland's approach was disproportionate and that less intrusive measures could achieve the same objectives.

Context of the Ruling

The Court examined whether Poland's practice complied with Article 15 of Directive 2014/24/EU, which allows exceptions for national security interests. These exceptions must be necessary and proportionate to justify the exclusion of competition.

III. THE COURT'S LEGAL ASSESSMENT

Restrictive Interpretation of Exceptions

- The Court reaffirmed that exceptions to competitive procurement rules must be interpreted restrictively.
- Member States cannot broadly claim national security concerns to bypass EU procurement obligations without concrete justification.

Application of Article 346(1)(a) TFEU

- Recognition of Security Interests: The Court acknowledged that Member States can define their essential security interests.
- Burden of Proof: However, Poland failed to demonstrate that open tender procedures could not safeguard these interests. The Court emphasized the need for concrete evidence, not general claims.

The Court found Poland's measures disproportionate because:

- The blanket exemption covered all sensitive documents, not just those with irreparable security implications.
- Alternatives, such as strict security standards or contractual clauses, could have met the security requirements without eliminating competition.

Exception for Specific Documents

- The Court accepted exceptions for certain documents (e.g., military or police IDs), where breaches could have severe, irreversible consequences for national security.
- However, Poland could not justify that all the documents in question required such treatment.

IV. ANALYSIS

Strengths and Weaknesses of the Ruling

Strengths:

- Reinforces that national security is a legitimate concern but must be narrowly interpreted.
- Clarifies that exceptions to EU rules require detailed evidence and proportionality.

Weaknesses:

- Creates challenges for states seeking centralized production of diverse sensitive documents, where security concerns are not equally critical for all.

Practical Implications

1. Selective Exceptions:
    o Member States must carefully evaluate which documents genuinely involve essential security interests and subject others to competitive procurement.

2. Security Standards in Tenders:
    o Competitive procurement can still accommodate security needs by incorporating stringent standards and clauses in tender documents.

Relevance for national arrangements

Distinction Between Security and General Public Interests

The judgment clarifies the boundary between essential security interests and broader public concerns, which must be addressed through procurement rules rather than exemptions.

Use of In-House Solutions

Public entities can still use in-house solutions under Article 12 of Directive 2014/24/EU, provided they meet the strict conditions for such arrangements.

Precedent value for other sectors

This ruling has implications for other sectors, such as defense and energy:

- Defense Procurement: Exceptions for defense-related contracts must demonstrate that open procedures would directly jeopardize security.
- Energy Infrastructure: Similar scrutiny applies to the use of state-owned entities for managing critical energy facilities.

Practical guidance for sensitive contracts

1. Define Security Requirements Clearly:
   - Include detailed confidentiality, security, and technical standards in tender documents.
2. Use Security Clauses in Contracts:
   - Include clauses that prohibit sharing sensitive information with third parties and specify strict data protection measures.
3. Restrict Competition Judiciously:
   - Use pre-qualification or closed tender procedures for contracts requiring heightened security.
4. Ensure Immutable Documentation:
   - Specify secure platforms for submitting immutable documentation to prevent alterations.
5. Alternative Evaluation Mechanisms:
   - Introduce security-specific scoring criteria or audits to assess bidders' capacity to handle sensitive contracts.
6. Cooperate with National Security Authorities:
   - Collaborate with security agencies to validate bidder qualifications and contract safeguards.
7. Justify Security Restrictions:
   - Document the necessity and proportionality of restrictions in the tendering process.
8. Adaptability for New Threats:

- Include clauses allowing for additional security measures if new risks emerge during the contract period.

V. CONCLUSION

This ruling underscores the importance of balancing national security concerns with the principles of competition and proportionality in public procurement. While exceptions for essential security interests are valid, they must be specific, justified, and narrowly applied. This ensures compliance with EU law while safeguarding both transparency and legitimate security needs.

- Choice of Law in the Use of International Purchasing Centralized Bodies

I. ESSENCE OF THE CASE

The case focuses on determining which national legal framework governs complaint procedures in public procurement when a central purchasing body (CPB) in one Member State conducts a procurement on behalf of a contracting authority in another Member State. The key issue is whether the law of the CPB's Member State or that of the contracting authority should apply to complaints.

II. FACTS OF THE CASE

Background

EVN Business Service (EBS), a CPB based in Austria, conducted a procurement procedure on behalf of Elektrorazpredelenie YUG (ER Yug), a contracting authority in Bulgaria. The procurement involved a framework agreement for electrical installations and construction work, divided into several lots.

The parties agreed to apply:

- Austrian law to the procurement process.
- Bulgarian law to the performance of the contract.

Issue

Two Bulgarian companies whose bids were rejected sought to challenge the procurement process. The regional administrative court in Niederösterreich, Austria, declared it lacked jurisdiction, arguing that the procurement fell under Bulgarian law due to the contracting authority's location.

Questions for the CJEU

1. Should complaint procedures be governed by the law of the CPB's Member State or that of the contracting authority's Member State?
2. Does this principle also apply to cross-border procurement?

III. THE COURT'S LEGAL ASSESSMENT

1. Framework for Assessment

- Article 57(3) of Directive 2014/24/EU: Governs situations where a contracting authority uses a CPB in another Member State. It specifies that the procedural rules of the CPB's Member State apply to the procurement process.
- Directive 89/665/EEC (Remedies Directive): Mandates that suppliers must have access to effective remedies in public procurement disputes.

The Court considered whether the procedural rules of the CPB's Member State include the applicable complaint procedures.

2. Application of Article 57(3)

The Court ruled that:

- The substantive and procedural rules of the CPB's Member State govern the entire procurement process, including complaint procedures.
- The complaint mechanisms must be handled under the CPB's national law to ensure consistency and legal certainty.

3. Justifications for the Court's Interpretation

- Uniform Application of Rules:

  Applying the CPB's national law to both procurement procedures and complaint mechanisms ensures legal clarity and equal treatment of bidders. Fragmented rules could lead to inconsistencies and unfair treatment.

- Efficiency and Transparency:

  Centralizing jurisdiction in the CPB's Member State provides a clear path for bidders to seek remedies. This avoids confusion about where and how complaints should be filed.

- Role of the CPB:

  Since the CPB controls the procurement process, its national legal framework is naturally suited to handle any disputes arising from the process.

4. The Court's Conclusion

- Complaints related to the procurement procedure in cross-border settings must be governed by the law of the CPB's Member State.
- In this case, Austrian law applies to the complaint procedures, and the competent Austrian court must address the matter.

IV. ANALYSIS

1. Strengthening Cross-Border Procurement

- Clarity and Simplicity: The ruling reinforces the principle that a single legal framework should govern cross-border procurement.

- Facilitating Supplier Participation: By ensuring consistent rules, the decision encourages suppliers from different Member States to participate without fear of legal ambiguity.

2. Ensuring Access to Remedies

- The decision eliminates potential jurisdictional conflicts, ensuring suppliers know where to file complaints.
- However, it requires contracting authorities in the supplier's Member State to accept limited oversight of procurement conducted by foreign CPBs.

3. Implications for National Procurement Authorities

1. Use of Foreign CPBs

- Contracting authorities engaging foreign CPBs must recognize that the procurement process and related complaints will be governed by the CPB's national law.
- Authorities must ensure clear agreements on jurisdiction and procedural rules.

2. Handling Shared Responsibilities

If responsibilities for the procurement process are shared between the CPB and the contracting authority:

- The law of the Member State with primary control over the decision-making process will likely apply.
- Complaints must address the origin of the contested action or decision.

3. Potential Obstacles for Local Suppliers

Barriers to Participation

- Language Barriers: Complaint mechanisms in a foreign language may deter local suppliers.
- Legal Complexity: Navigating an unfamiliar legal system may discourage smaller suppliers from filing complaints.
- Increased Costs: Higher legal and administrative costs may dissuade local suppliers from challenging decisions.

4. Measures to Mitigate Barriers

- Clear Guidelines: CPBs and contracting authorities should specify applicable laws, complaint procedures, and jurisdiction in tender documents.
- Language Support: Providing key documents and instructions in multiple languages can enhance accessibility.
- Digital Tools: Online platforms for complaint submission can simplify processes for suppliers from different Member States.
- Training and Outreach: Workshops or informational sessions can prepare local suppliers to engage in cross-border procurement.

4. Practical Recommendations

For Contracting Authorities

- Clearly state applicable laws for procurement and complaint procedures in tender documents.
- Collaborate with CPBs to provide comprehensive information to bidders.

For CPBs

- Ensure compliance with the Remedies Directive by providing accessible and efficient complaint mechanisms.
- Offer guidance to suppliers on navigating the legal system of the CPB's Member State.

For Suppliers

- Verify applicable laws and jurisdiction for complaints before submitting bids.
- Seek legal counsel familiar with the CPB's national legal framework.

IV. CONCLUSION

The CJEU's ruling in C-480/22 reinforces the principle that the legal framework of the CPB's Member State governs both the procurement process and related complaints in cross-border public procurement. This ensures consistency and legal clarity but highlights the need for measures to support local suppliers in navigating foreign complaint systems. The decision underscores the importance of clear agreements and transparency in cross-border procurement collaborations.

8. C-441/22 and C-443/22, Judgments of 7 December 2023

I. ESSENCE OF THE CASE

The judgment addresses whether extending contract deadlines without formal written agreement or valid justification due to unforeseen circumstances constitutes a substantial modification in violation of the EU Public Procurement Directive (2014/24/EU). The case raises key principles of transparency, equal treatment, and the necessity of formal agreements for altering contract terms.

II. FACTS OF THE CASE

1. Background of the Contract

A public contract for construction and infrastructure works was awarded by a contracting authority in Bulgaria. The project was co-financed by EU Structural Funds, with strict deadlines to qualify for funding. The original contract specified a fixed completion deadline.

2. Extension of Deadlines Without Formal Agreement

During the execution of the contract, significant delays occurred. These delays were implicitly accepted by both parties through practical conduct, but no formal amendment to the contract was documented.

The contracting authority argued that the delays were due to external factors, including administrative obstacles and seasonal work restrictions near coastal areas.

3. Funding Review

A Bulgarian oversight authority reviewed the contract and determined that the deadline extensions constituted a substantial modification.

The authority imposed a 25% financial penalty, citing breaches of transparency and equal treatment principles.

4. Dispute

The contracting authority contested this decision, claiming the delays were justified under Article 72(1)(c) of Directive 2014/24/EU, which allows modifications for unforeseen circumstances. However, the oversight body argued that these conditions were neither unforeseen nor documented in writing.

The case was referred to the CJEU for clarification on:

1. Whether the extensions constituted a substantial modification.
2. Whether the circumstances qualified as unforeseen under the directive.
3. Whether formal written agreements are mandatory for valid contract amendments.

III. LEGAL ASSESSMENT BY THE CJEU

1. Substantial Modification of the Contract (Article 72(1), Directive 2014/24/EU)

Interpretation:

Any modification that materially alters the balance of the contract or impacts essential terms such as deadlines constitutes a substantial modification.

Application:

The Court held that the extensions materially altered the contract's essence since the deadlines were core elements of the procurement process.

The lack of formal agreement excluded other potential bidders from competing on equal terms, violating transparency and equal treatment principles.

Written Agreement Requirement

Interpretation:

While the directive does not explicitly mandate written documentation for every modification, written agreements are essential for transparency and accountability.

Application:

The absence of a formal written amendment undermined the ability to verify compliance with proportionality and equal treatment.

The parties' informal conduct was insufficient to justify changes, as it failed to provide a clear, auditable trail of decision-making.

3. Unforeseen Circumstances (Article 72(1)(c))

The court assessed what constitutes unforeseen circumstances that may justify contract modifications. The conditions must be:

- Criteria for Unforeseen Circumstances:
    1. Unpredictable by a diligent contracting authority.
    2. Beyond the parties' control.
    3. Proportional to the required modifications.

- Application:
    - The Court ruled that administrative delays and seasonal work restrictions were foreseeable and should have been accounted for in the original contract terms.
    - These factors did not qualify as unforeseen circumstances under Article 72(1)(c).

IV. LEGAL PRINCIPLES ESTABLISHED

1. Substantial Modifications

Changes to fundamental contract terms, such as deadlines, must comply with procurement rules and avoid giving undue advantage to any party.

2. Written Agreements

All significant modifications require formal written documentation to ensure transparency and facilitate review.

3. Unforeseen Circumstances

Only truly unpredictable and uncontrollable events can justify modifications under Article 72(1)(c). Routine administrative or operational challenges are insufficient.

V. ANALYSIS

The boundary between what requires written documentation and what can be accepted through actions in public contracts depends on several factors based on EU law principles and the interpretation of the Procurement Directive. Here are some key points to help understand this boundary:

1. **General Requirement for Written Documentation**
    - o **Principle**: Written documentation is crucial to ensure transparency, accountability, and equal treatment of tenderers. This is particularly important when changes might affect the competitive basis or give one party an undue advantage.
    - o **Exception**: If the change is insignificant and does not affect competition, actions or implied consent may be accepted in rare cases.

2. **What Does the Directive (2014/24/EU) Say?**
    - o **Article 72 (Substantial Changes)**: All substantial changes must be documented in writing and follow the directive's procedures.
    - o **Non-Substantial Changes**: Minor changes that do not affect the original balance between the parties or the competition conditions may sometimes be accepted without written documentation.

3. **Substantial vs. Non-Substantial Changes**
    - o **Substantial Changes**: Changes affecting fundamental elements of the contract, such as price, delivery time, or qualification requirements, always require written agreement.
    - o **Non-Substantial Changes**: Technical or operational changes that do not impact other parties' ability to compete may sometimes be handled without written documentation, but this must be justified.

4. **When Can Actions Be Sufficient?**

- o **Clear Agreement Between Parties**: If both parties agree on a minor change, and this can be documented through emails, correspondence, or other forms of communication, it may be accepted in some cases.
- o **No Impact on Competition**: If the change does not affect the competitive basis or create advantages for one party that others did not have the opportunity to compete for, actions may be sufficient.

5. **Court's Assessment in This Case**
- o The EU Court pointed out that the lack of written documentation in the case rendered the change non-verifiable and undermined transparency. Actions alone were therefore not accepted as sufficient in this case.
- o The court suggested that even minor changes should be documented in writing to ensure compliance with the requirements for equal treatment and transparency.

What Should Procuring Entities Include in Tender Documents to Ensure Flexibility in Unforeseen Circumstances Without Violating Procurement Rules?

1. **Include Explicit Modification Clauses**
- o **Purpose**: Allow necessary contract modifications without triggering a new competition requirement.
- o **Content of the Clause**:
  - ▪ Precise conditions for when and how changes can be made.
  - ▪ Types of permissible changes (e.g., deadline adjustments, minor technical modifications).
  - ▪ Requirement that changes must be proportionate and justified.
  - ▪ Relevant provisions in the directive: Article 72(1)(a), allowing changes clearly specified in the tender documents.

2. **Define What Constitutes Unforeseen Circumstances**
   - o **Purpose**: Avoid ambiguity about which situations can justify changes.
   - o **Specifications**:
     - Examples of qualifying events (e.g., natural disasters, new regulatory requirements, external delays).
     - Method for documenting and assessing the unpredictability of circumstances.
     - Relevant provisions in the directive: Article 72(1)(c), addressing unforeseen circumstances beyond the control of the contracting authority.

3. **Include Flexible Deadline and Performance Clauses**
   - o **Purpose**: Manage delays and changes in delivery conditions without breaching rules.
   - o **Content of the Clause**:
     - Provisions for deadline extensions under specific conditions (e.g., force majeure).
     - Mechanisms for renegotiating deadlines based on documented needs.
   - o **Benefit**: Allows adjustments without being considered a substantial change.

4. **Require Written Documentation for All Changes**
   - o **Purpose**: Ensure transparency and accountability.
   - o **Content of the Clause**:
     - All changes must be documented in writing and approved by both parties.
     - Requirements for how changes should be recorded and reported.

- o **Benefit**: Prevents disputes over informal changes that cannot be substantiated.

5. **Implement Review Clauses**
   - o **Purpose**: Allow evaluation and adjustment of the contract at specific milestones.
   - o **Content of the Clause**:
     - Provisions for periodic reviews of contract performance.
     - Scope for minor adjustments based on the review, provided they are not substantial.
     - Relevant provisions in the directive: Article 72(1)(e), allowing non-substantial changes.

6. **Clarify Conflict Resolution Mechanisms**
   - o **Purpose**: Prevent escalation of disputes related to modifications.
   - o **Content of the Clause**:
     - Procedure for resolving disagreements on the interpretation of modification clauses.
     - Reference to independent mediation or arbitration bodies that can be used.

7. **Consider Use of Standards and Guidelines**
   - o **Purpose**: Ensure the contract complies with relevant laws and regulations.
   - o **What to Include**:
     - Reference to applicable standards for force majeure, working conditions, and other relevant areas.

8. **Include Clear Price Adjustment Clauses**
   - ○ **Purpose**: Manage economic changes (e.g., inflation, commodity prices).
   - ○ **Content of the Clause**:
     - ▪ Conditions for when and how prices can be adjusted.
     - ▪ Methods for calculating adjustments based on objective criteria.

9. **Use Explicit Language**
   - ○ **Purpose**: Reduce the risk of misinterpretation.
   - ○ **Recommendations**:
     - ▪ Avoid vague or general wording.
     - ▪ Use clear and precise terms to describe the conditions for changes.

Summary

By including explicit clauses for modifications, defining unforeseen circumstances, and ensuring written documentation and accountability, contracting authorities can balance the need for flexibility with the requirement to comply with procurement rules. This approach will help reduce the risk of disputes and financial corrections while upholding the principles of equal treatment and transparency.

.

- Rejection due to serious misconduct raising doubts about the supplier's integrity
- Requirement for independent assessment by the contracting authority

I. THE ESSENCE OF THE CASE

The case concerns whether an economic operator can be excluded from participating in a public procurement procedure due to anti-competitive behavior in previous tenders, and whether national authorities can transfer the decision-making authority regarding such exclusions exclusively to competition authorities.

Should the assessment of an operator's reliability and integrity, including possible "self-cleaning" measures, rest solely with the competition authority, or must the contracting authority conduct an independent assessment?

II. THE FACTS OF THE CASE

Background of the tender procedure:

Infraestruturas de Portugal, a Portuguese public contracting authority in the railway sector, announced a tender for the supply of creosote-treated wooden materials. The contract was awarded to Futrifer, a company that had previously been fined for participating in anti-competitive agreements.

<u>Toscca's complaint:</u>

A competitor, Toscca, challenged the contract award. They argued that Futrifer did not meet the integrity and reliability requirements imposed on economic operators and that the company's prior anti-competitive behavior should have resulted in its exclusion.

<u>Portuguese legislation:</u>

Under Portuguese law, an economic operator can only be excluded from public procurement if a national competition authority has explicitly imposed a sanction prohibiting the operator from participating in future tenders. In this case, there was no such explicit sanction against Futrifer.

Actions by the contracting authority: Infraestruturas de Portugal did not independently assess Futrifer's reliability but justified the award on the grounds that there was no legal basis for exclusion under national law.

<u>Questions to the Court of Justice of the European Union:</u>

The Portuguese court referred the following questions to the CJEU:

- Is it consistent with Directive 2014/24/EU for a contracting authority to delegate the entire assessment of exclusion grounds to the competition authority?
- Does the contracting authority have an independent obligation to assess an operator's reliability and integrity, even when prior conduct may have undermined confidence in the operator?
- Is the competition authority's decision sufficient, or must the contracting authority assess the operator's "self-cleaning" measures before making an award decision?

The case thus highlights the relationship between national rules, the EU Directive, and the obligation to assess an operator's integrity in public procurement procedures.

III. THE COURT'S ASSESSMENT

The Court's evaluations, interpretations, legal principles, and applications:

The CJEU analyzed the case under Directive 2014/24/EU, particularly Article 57, which governs discretionary exclusion grounds for economic operators. The Court addressed several aspects concerning the obligations and authority of contracting entities, as well as the interplay between national law and EU legal principles.

1. Obligation to implement discretionary exclusion grounds
     - Interpretation: The Court emphasized that Member States are obliged to implement the discretionary exclusion grounds provided by the Directive into national law. This includes Article 57(4)(d), which allows contracting authorities to exclude suppliers for previous serious misconduct affecting their integrity, such as participation in anti-competitive agreements.
     - Legal principle: Member States cannot restrict this provision to apply only after an explicit decision by competition authorities. Contracting entities must have the authority to conduct an independent assessment of the supplier's integrity.

2. The contracting authority's independent assessment obligation
     - Interpretation: The Directive imposes an independent obligation on contracting entities to assess whether an operator meets the requirements for integrity and reliability, even in cases where national authorities have not explicitly mandated exclusion.
     - Application: The Court held that Infraestruturas de Portugal, by failing to conduct an independent assessment

of Futrifer despite the company's prior violations, acted in violation of the Directive's requirements.

- o Legal principle: The competition authority's evaluation may serve as guidance, but the contracting authority must independently conduct a concrete and proportional assessment of the operator's reliability in the specific procurement.

3. "Self-cleaning" measures
   - o Interpretation: The Court highlighted that economic operators have the right to present evidence of measures taken to restore their integrity ("self-cleaning" measures). Contracting authorities must assess these measures under Article 57(6).
   - o Application: Although Futrifer had the opportunity to present such measures, the responsibility lay with the contracting authority to evaluate whether the measures were adequate. The failure to assess these measures constituted a breach of the Directive.

4. Principle of proportionality
   - o Interpretation: Any exclusion must be proportional and based on a comprehensive assessment of the operator's reliability. The contracting authority must consider the severity of the prior violation and the circumstances surrounding it.
   - o Application: The Court pointed out that Portuguese law, by excluding proportionality assessments from the contracting authority's responsibilities, restricts the application of the Directive and is therefore inconsistent with EU law.

5. Principles of equal treatment and transparency
   - o Interpretation: Contracting authorities must ensure that all operators are treated equally and that decisions regarding exclusion or award are transparent. By failing to consider Futrifer's past behavior and measures to restore integrity, the contracting authority jeopardized these principles.
   - o Legal principle: EU law requires that all operators receive fair and equal treatment and that decisions are clearly justified.

6. Conclusion
   - o Court's decision: The CJEU concluded that Portuguese law, as applied in this case, does not comply with Directive 2014/24/EU. Contracting authorities must have independent authority to assess the reliability and integrity of economic operators, regardless of the decisions of competition authorities.
   - o Legal principle: Article 57 of the Directive grants contracting authorities both the obligation and the right to conduct independent evaluations, and national legislation must allow for this.

IV: PRACTICAL SIGNIFICANCE OF THE JUDGMENT

This judgment clarifies that:

- The competition authority's decision is not definitive but advisory:

   The contracting authority cannot rely solely on the absence of explicit sanctions from competition authorities. Instead, it must independently assess an economic operator's integrity.

- Contracting authorities must actively evaluate integrity and "self-cleaning" measures:

  Authorities cannot defer their duty to competition authorities but must review the operator's specific circumstances and any corrective measures taken.

- National law must align with the Directive's requirements for flexibility and proportionality:

  Member States must ensure their national frameworks allow contracting entities to conduct proportional, independent assessments.

V. SUMMARY

Contracting authorities must independently evaluate the integrity of economic operators, regardless of whether past violations occurred in a different procurement. Authorities must be empowered to impose exclusions if necessary.

Key takeaways for national contracting entities:

1. Real, independent assessments are mandatory: Contracting authorities must base their decisions on credible indications that an economic operator has participated in anti-competitive agreements or other misconduct. This responsibility cannot be delegated solely to other authorities.
2. Prior anti-competitive behavior is relevant for new procurements:
   A lack of explicit sanctions from competition authorities does

not absolve the contracting authority from conducting its own assessment.
3. Compliance with principles of good administration, proportionality, and transparency is crucial: Authorities must justify their decisions thoroughly and ensure they are balanced, fair, and transparent.

VI. ANALYSIS

What happens if a contracting authority and a competition authority have differing assessments of whether self-cleaning measures are sufficient?

If a contracting authority and a competition authority disagree on whether self-cleaning measures are sufficient, several legal and practical challenges arise. EU Court jurisprudence and Directive 2014/24/EU provide guidance on handling such situations:

1. **Independent Assessment Duty of the Contracting Authority**
   - **Directive Requirement**: Article 57(6) of Directive 2014/24/EU obliges contracting authorities to assess self-cleaning measures independently of other authorities' assessments. The contracting authority is responsible for determining whether the measures are sufficient to restore the supplier's integrity in the specific competition.
   - **Implication**: Even if the competition authority previously deemed the measures insufficient, the contracting authority may reach a different conclusion based on updated evidence or specific requirements of the competition.
2. **Advisory Role of Competition Authorities**
   - **Guidance, Not Binding**: Assessments by competition authorities regarding a supplier's reliability and measures against past violations can guide the

contracting authority but are not binding. The contracting authority must base its decision on the context and requirements of the current tender.

- ○ **Risk of Conflict**: Significant discrepancies between assessments can lead to complaints from suppliers or other interested parties, alleging that the contracting authority failed to fulfill its duty to act independently.

3. **Principle of Proportionality**

- ○ **Proportional Assessment**: The contracting authority's decision must be proportional and based on a holistic evaluation of the self-cleaning measures, including their relevance, implementation, and effectiveness.
- ○ **Subsidiary Role of Competition Authorities**: While competition authorities may provide information on past violations, the contracting authority bears its own responsibility to balance equal treatment, competition, and integrity considerations.

How can suppliers who believe they have been unfairly excluded ensure their complaints are handled fairly and effectively?

- **Supplier's Right to Appeal**: If a supplier believes the contracting authority has unreasonably rejected or accepted self-cleaning measures, the decision can be challenged through appeal procedures.
- **Judicial Review**: A national complaints body or court can assess whether the contracting authority fulfilled its obligations under the directive and whether the evaluation of the measures was adequately justified and proportional.

Best Methods for Documenting and Justifying Such Evaluations to Ensure Transparency and Avoid Complaints

To ensure transparency and minimize complaints, evaluations of supplier integrity and self-cleaning measures should be documented and justified systematically and thoroughly. Here are the best practices:

1. **Follow Established Procedures and Requirements**
   - Include the discretionary exclusion grounds in the tender documentation so they are known to suppliers in advance.
2. **Develop a Standardized Evaluation Template**
   - Use a template or checklist to ensure all relevant aspects of integrity and self-cleaning measures are assessed consistently for all suppliers.
   - Assign points or levels for various factors, such as the severity of past violations, the content of the measures, and the degree of compliance.
3. **Ensure Transparency in the Evaluation Process**
   - **Justification**: Explain how each factor was assessed.
   - **Written Documentation**: Maintain detailed notes describing the evaluation process and decisions for each supplier, including references to relevant facts and documents.
4. **Leverage Third-Party Evaluations and Guidance**
   - **Expert Assistance**: Consult legal advisors or competition authorities, especially in complex cases, to enhance the legitimacy of the evaluation.
   - **External Audits**: If possible, involve an independent party to validate the evaluation process.
5. **Systematically Document Self-Cleaning Measures**
   - **Information Gathering**: Require detailed documentation from suppliers showing the measures implemented to restore integrity (e.g., leadership changes, new policies, training, or internal audits).

- o **Evaluation of Measures**: Explain how the measures address past violations and why they are deemed sufficient or insufficient.

6. **Ensure Proportionality in Evaluations**
   - o **Balancing Act**: Weigh the severity of past violations against the effectiveness of the measures. Justify why the decision is proportional to the nature of the violation and the risk of future breaches.
   - o **Example-Based Arguments**: Provide examples of similar cases to demonstrate that the evaluation aligns with past practices.

7. **Involve Stakeholders in the Process**
   - o **Right to Respond**: Allow suppliers to comment on the evaluation before the final decision is made. This strengthens legal certainty and reduces the likelihood of complaints.
   - o **Dialogue**: Ensure stakeholders understand the evaluation criteria and receive explanations of how the evaluation was conducted.

8. **Justify and Clearly Communicate the Decision**
   - o **Decision Letter**: Prepare a written decision letter summarizing the evaluation and justifying the conclusion with references to the tender documentation, directives, and facts of the case.
   - o **Clarify Appeal Options**: Inform suppliers of their right to appeal and how to do so.

9. **Establish a Robust Archival Structure**
   - o **Document Storage**: Retain all evaluation documents, correspondence, and notes in a structured archive for future reference or audits.
   - o **Traceability**: Ensure all evaluations can be traced back to responsible individuals or committees.

10. **Learn from Previous Complaints**

- **Analyze Complaints**: Review past complaints and decisions by complaints bodies to identify weaknesses in the evaluation process.

- **Adjust Procedures**: Refine evaluation methods based on lessons learned from previous cases.

-